My African

POEMS FOR YOUNGER READERS
COMPILED BY ROBIN MALAN

David Philip Publishers
Cape Town Johannesburg

First published in South Africa by David Philip Publishers (Pty) Ltd, 208 Werdmuller Centre, Claremont, 7700, South Africa

ISBN 0-86486-312-8

Grateful acknowledgements are due to Orde Levinson and to the John Muafangejo Trust for permission to reproduce details from illustrations published in *The African Dream: Visions of Love and Sorrow: The Art of John Muafangejo* (Thames and Hudson, 1992). The illustrations are listed on page viii.

Printed by FormsXpress, Unit 1, Futura 15, Barker Road, Retreat, 7945, South Africa

Contents

At Play

My Family

Other People

Places

Inside Me

Animals

List of illustrations
(Reproduced from *The African Dream: Visions of Love and Sorrow: The Art of John Muafangejo* by Orde Levinson)

At School, opposite p. 1
(Detail from no. 47 Our Church at Rorke's Drift, 1968)
At Play, opposite p. 29
(Detail from no. 99 Lonely Man, Man of Man, 1974)
Other People, opposite p. 65
(Detail from no. 49 New Archbishop Desmond Tutu enthroned, 1986)
Places, opposite p. 92
(No. 73 Holiday, 1983)
Animals, opposite p. 129
(No. 40 Etosha Pan Wild Life, 1982)

Introduction

The world is full of interesting things. People, mainly. And animals. And places and times and things to do and see and hear ... and think about, and feel about. One of the best ways to think and feel about our world is to read and to write poems about ourselves and our world. That way we find we are thinking and feeling in ways we haven't done before. And we're working − and playing − with words and sounds and language in new and different ways. All of that is exciting.

In some ways all of this is more exciting for us than for other people, because we're in Africa. And Africa is just full of all sorts of interest and excitement. There really can't be many places in the world that offer as much as Africa does to those who want to find out as much about life as they can.

All of the poems in this book are by Africans, all sorts of different Africans, from many parts of Africa, though most are from Southern Africa, and most of those are from South Africa. About half of the poems collected here were written when the writers were at school. So, both in time and place, the poems should be close to you.

You'll see that the poems are collected under a number of headings: *At School*, *At Home*, and so on. That way you can read poems that are different ways of looking at similar things. But, also, you'll enjoy just opening the book anywhere and trying out the poems you find there.

And, of course, it would be good if reading some of these poems made you want to try writing some poems yourself.

Whatever happens, hope you enjoy it!

RM
Cape Town

At School

Ignorance

Jeanette Isaacman
South Africa, b. 1958

What's a poem?
A poem!
Yes a poem.
Why! Everybody knows.
Knows what?
A poem.
Well I don't know.
You don't?
No I don't.
It'sathoughtwhichisputintowordsandwrittendowninver
sesandlinesanditsometimesrhymesanditsometimesdoesn't
I asked you what a poem is!!!

The Poet to His Readers

Ralph Bitamazire
Tanzania

Hear, hear this my poem!
Those who do not have any
Take mine,
Hear this thunder of victory,
The song of my ancestors:
My small Spear,
My poem.

Poem

Prashant Desai
Zambia, b. 1973

A poem is like a river
There are things
  deep down in the dark waters
Just like the meanings under the words

The words flow in one direction,
  smoothly and swiftly
Sometimes tumbling over a waterfall
And sometimes ending in a pool of understanding.

Verbs

Dele Olaniyi
Nigeria

A verb is the worst thing in the world,
For me to learn aright,
And when the teacher calls on me
I never get it right.

I try to give the parts of verbs
And say see, saw, seen.
But when I give the parts of be
I can't say bee, baw, been!

If I give the parts of go
And say go, went, gone,
It doesn't help a bit with grow!
I can't say grow, grent, grone.

The parts of take you're very sure
Are take and took and taken:
Yet bake is very wrong
as bake and book and baken.

One Day

Tyrone August
South Africa

i'm going to
pick up
all the commas
and semi-colons
and fullstops
i've ever used

roll them up
with all
the brackets
and hyphens
and colons

and all the
question marks
and inverted commas
and apostrophes

and throw
them all out again
as one
big
exclamation mark

Registering for School, 1936

Peter E Clarke
South Africa, b. 1926

That first day
he watched
his mother and teacher-to-be
put together necessary information.
He stood waiting
listening to the way
his particulars were given
as if, even though there,
he were elsewhere or dead or dumb.
When they were done
he asked his mother, "Can we go home now?"
"No," she said gently,
"You have to stay."
She didn't let him know
learning is a lifelong process
and on this journey
you've a long way to go
alone.

Sitting on a Rock

Nibor Nalam
South Africa, b. 1940

First day. New school. New country, even.
Not easy. I sit on a rock
as students drift from lunch.
Here come some white guys.
Can't talk to them –
my English is no good.
They vaguely nod and smile as they pass by.
Why did I even come here?
In Thembisa I knew lots of people
and lots of people knew me.
Here I haven't said a word to anyone.
Here comes a black guy on his own.
I've got to try.
"Heyta, mfowethu … ek sê, heyta …"
"Like I'm real sorry man, I'mfrom the States,
and hey I don' speak any African languages."
Oh no.
Now what am I going to do,
he's sitting down beside me on the rock!
"So anyway, how's it goin'?
You reckon you gonna like it here?"
I turn and see his easy smile,
his unjudging eyes.
"Ja," I'm smiling back at him,
"I'm very much happy to be here."

Days

Michele Freind
South Africa, b.1952

wednesday is dreamday
dullday tiredday
need a holiday
thinking of saturday

saturday is stanleyday
townday dateday
needed a funday
thinking of sunday

sunday is sleepday
beachday eatday
needed a coolday
thinking of schoolday

Jealousy

Kathryn Phelan
South Africa

A new girl came,
I don't know her name,
But then all things changed.
Where were my friends?
Why did they go?
I don't know.

Poem: the School Bus

Colin Sentongo
Uganda, b. 1974

At the bus stop I did arrive,
People moved like bees in a hive.

I turned and heard a clatter and a "Peep",
And there came the bus all in a heap.

We all ran on to get a seat,
But none of the others could I beat.

But there sat Mike with a very big frown,
Shouting, "Hey people, come on, move down."

The engine started with a bang,
And the bus moved forward with a clang.

It rumbled and shook, and the birds began to hover,
While pedestrians turned and ran for cover.

The bus slowed down with a screeching halt,
We had arrived without a fault.

This is the end of my poem about the bus.
I hope no one makes a very big fuss.

To a Class of Test-Writers

Karen Press
South Africa, b.1956

squirm, worms
pinned down to your seats
by a piece of paper
stretch, scratch, crack your fingers
screw up eyes, scribble
stop, stare
sigh
look at me
I am a blank wall
between you and the answer

squirm, worms
if the paper holds you down
I won't free you
the wall is between us
you could climb over
if your wormy little bodies had the strength

I Hear Silent Steps

Acelio Ruface
Mozambique, b. 1973

I hear silent steps
The steps of a Mozambican child
Going to school
With worn-out shoes
Which show his toes
With few exercise-books and books
With no sweater
To protect himself from the cold.

A Mozambican child
Though
In his eyes
There is a garden of tears,
In his hands
He holds a pen and a piece of paper
He goes to school.

I hear silent steps
The steps of a child
Whose eyes
Are like the eyes of a kite
Which can see
Far, far places.

School Visit

Nibor Nalam
South Africa, b.1940

Today's the best day at school
The actors are coming!
We've walked in lines to the hall
We're sitting cross-legged in a big circle
in the middle of the floor
I like it when they act in the middle of us
and not on the stage
Maybe they'll ask us to help them
Like last time we went on a journey
inside the bloodstream
We went on a Lub Dub Safari
We were all the organs of the body
spread out around the hall
I was in the Digestive System
We were a sausage machine that made sausages
and passed them on to the Excretory System
Yuck! It was fun
The time before we were amaXhosa
when Nongqawuse came and told us
what she'd heard and seen down by the river
and how we had to kill our cattle
and then we died
That one was sad
I wonder what today's will be?
Miss says it's called Gold Rush
and Miss told us all about Pilgrim's Rest
Maybe we'll go and dig for gold
Maybe I can be the robber in the
Robber's Grave facing the wrong way
Maybe ... maybe ...
Here they come!

As I Went Home from School

Colin Dalziel
South Africa, b. 1955

As I went home from school one day,
I saw a small tough-looking boy,
Who looked at me as if I were his prey.
His eyes stared so very
Grey.
He wore a leather jacket
And on its back it had "Ray".
I wanted to turn and walk away,
But I didn't have the nerve.
He came straight for me.
My body started to shiver,
My knees to quiver.
Ten paces away the sweat was
Trickling down my face.
Then like a cow and with its grace,
He walked away.

At Home

The House

Seitlhamo Motsapi
South Africa, b. 1966

the little man
with hands like the hide
of an impatient alligator
tells me he built his house smaller
so the nights in winter
could be warmer

i shake my head softly
& say love would have been kept out
by many walls

as it is
when they tire from wandering
through an indifferent world
all the suns come to sleep
in this house

Inside My Zulu Hut

Mbuyiseni Oswald Mtshali
South Africa, b.1940

It is a hive
without any bees
to build the walls
with golden bricks of honey.
A cave cluttered
with a millstone,
calabashes of sour milk
claypots of foaming beer
sleeping grass mats
wooden head-rests
tanned goatskins
tied with riempies
to wattle rafters
blackened by the smoke
of kneaded cow-dung
burning under
the three-legged pot
on the earthen floor
to cook my porridge.

Oupa's Chair

Peter E Clarke
South Africa, b. 1926

Not even throne-like,
the seat of Oupa's seniority,
in his lifetime
no one would dare to place himself
on that particular patriarchal chair.

Small Bench

Peter E Clarke
South Africa, b. 1926

This perefienboks bankie
is the right height
on which to sit comfortably,
reach down with scissors
and trim toenails
easily.

Or on which to sit on the stoep outside
and watch the evening gently coming on
and watch the shepherds
and their flocks of sheep
come home.

This bankie is just right,
the height,
on which to sit and think
your thoughts
at odd times through the day.

Bookshelf

Peter E Clarke
South Africa, b. 1926

Just look here!
Who says
a tamatiekissie bookshelf
will not bear
the weight combined
of Bible wisdom, religious tracts,
informative books
and even dog-eared paperbacks? '

An Old Uncle's Vegetable Garden

Daniel Stolfi
South Africa, b. 1956

A row of tomato plants
held up by slipshod home-made dowels
& tied fast by strips of black cloth
grows lengthwise along the fence.

Baby marrows, lettuce, carrots,
beans and cabbage
grow in nine beds
each a metre-by-three.
Rows of working space between them.

Spinach is planted & watered
in a newly raked bed.
The gathered onions
that previously grew there
are left in the sun to dry out,
filling three boxes.

Hoe, rake, spade, wheel-barrow
and watering-can.
The working tools lean against the wall
at the end of the day.

Old Ouma Murray's Keys

adapted from Hylda Mary Richards
Zimbabwe, 1898–1978

The house is in confusion, the kids run to and fro,
There's rummaging in cupboards and there's hunting high
  and low;
And what is the excitement and hurry, if you please?
The answer is: "They're looking for old Ouma Murray's keys!"

"Wherever have they got to?" she says with wrinkled brow.
"I left them on the table and they've simply vanished now!"
So Aunt must leave her baking and get down on her knees –
She's searching under things to find old Ouma Murray's keys.

She says she can't explain it, just how they disappear:
Perhaps when she went visiting she might have left them there!
So hurry, send the grandchildren at once to Mrs B's,
To ask if she has chanced to find old Ouma Murray's keys.

Then Oupa comes and mutters, "What, lost your keys once
  more?
Where do you think you put them? Are they still stuck in the
  door?"
Advice is all he offers and helpful words like these:
"Why ever do you want to go and lose the blooming keys?"

Old Ouma Murray's crying, she doesn't like to tell,
But now she feels quite certain that she's lost her specs as well!
And all the while the mother hen is sitting at her ease
On thirteen tiny chickens and old Ouma Murray's keys!

The Burglar

Trevor Lubbe
South Africa

he came stealthily . . .
but i heard him.
they were asleep,
both of them.
and i thought . . .
"Why is he trying to get in?"
i've been trying seven years
to get out.

I Saw Her There One Day

Robert van der Valk
South Africa, b. 1951

i saw her there one day;
in our christmas tree
(which we had thrown out the previous week).
she hung there on a string;
a little girl
with a dress that glittered gold and silver.
and she moved
with each breath of air,
and tumbled and twisted in a whirl.

it rained that night
and the next morning she was gone.

Fear

B N Brink
South Africa

A dark room when I was seven –
"Don't shut the door, leave it half-open."
Angry voices in the kitchen –
A liquid fear flowing into wider streams.

Suns

Beverley Abel
South Africa, b. 1954

the room was bare
empty
and cold
then you came
holding a bunch of marigolds
in your hand
which you kept behind your back.
you placed the flowers
in an empty coffee tin
on the window-sill
and sun rushed in
bringing warmth
through the frozen pane.

Okombahe

Elizabeth Khaxas
Zimbabwe

i remember the
warm nights
in which the
river glowed like a silver snake
and my feet finding their way to it

standing in the lukewarm
water which flowed past my feet
looking up at the moon and stars
and the date palms waving
in the fine breeze
and me feeling so warm and safe
in the soft darkness of the evening
lost in the magic of water, sand and stars
till mother's call would
come surprisingly to my ears

to draw me away
to another world
of never-ending stories
in the little hut near the river

"Cookology" First, Biology Second

Ilda Maria
Mozambique, b. 1972

Mother: Carlaaaaaa! Carlaaaaaa!
      Where are you going, my daughter?
      Don't you see
      That it's too hot?

Carla: Mum, I'm going to school
      I'm going to learn
      How to read and write.

Mother: Carla, Carla my daughter
      You have learnt enough
      Now even biology you know by heart
      But you ...

Carla: Yes, mum
      I'm sorry to cut you short
      I know what you mean.

Mother: Carla, my daughter
      You shame me your mother
      Now you're big enough
      To be a mother.

Carla: Mum, I know what you mean
      What I must learn now
      Or what I should have learnt
      Long before I learnt biology
      Is "cookology", "sweepology",
      And "washology".

Hey, Man, I'm the Same Mpho!

Nibor Nalam
South Africa, b. 1940

Term's been good, though long
Highveld Swazi winter fine and sharp
Now it's PE, home and holidays

All term, with tray in hand, I stand and queue
chatting to whoever happens to be around
Then turn and sit any old where
and chat to whoever happens to be there

At Jan Smuts my flight's not due
So time to grab some lunch
Once more, tray in hand, I stand and queue
Then turn and sit just where there's space

Someone pushes the pause-button:
Two white men
forks in mid-air
jaws in mid-chew
stare, bug-eyed, at me

The reel continues, in slow-mo now:
Two white men
forks down
trays up
stand, and move to a table over there

A twelve-week term drops broken
on the floor beside me

The Fade of Day

Louise Eyeington
Swaziland, b. 1968

Pull myself
On to the window ledge
To watch the night
Crawl like a cautious
Child over the hills
And to feel the wind
Which gently moves the clouds
      Making space
      For the stars

If a Star Stirs...

Heather Robertson
South Africa, b. 1964

if a star
broke away from
the great blanket of night
and popped onto your pillow
would you spin into its arms
or would you turn your head and sleep?

My Strange Room

Nonhlanhla Shembe Williams
Lesotho, b. 1968

My room
splashed with bright colours,
  My cell
slashed with white bars,
  My comfort
during moments of torment,
  My hell
during minutes of happiness.

So strange,
that it should be that way,
and perhaps better to say,
  My room
slashed with white bars,
  My cell
splashed with bright colours,
  My comfort
during moments of happiness,
  My hell
during moments of torment,
  My strange room
and cell in one.

Beds

Karen Press
South Africa, b. 1956

this is
her side of the bed
and someone else
is sleeping

24

on my side
of another bed
so it goes

both of us wishing
we were back in the places
we stayed so warm, so long, so lovely
booted out
now we're climbing into other beds
full of ghosts

I'm making up a bed inside my head
clean sheets plenty of pillows
there I'm going to curl up holding tight
whoever I want
noone's ever going to make me leave

Into Sleep

Jeremy Gordin
South Africa, b. 1952

Night air
                        quivering
nosed icily inwards.
The moon
                        making bars
                        upon the bed
enfolded me
in mist

and I slept.

Palm Leaves of Childhood

G Adali-Morti
Ghana

When I was very small indeed,
and Joe and Fred were six-year giants.
my father, they and I, with soil
did mix farmyard manure.
In this we planted coconuts,
naming them by brothers' names.
The palms grew faster far than I;
and soon, ere I could grow a Man,
they, flowering, reached their goal!
Like the ear-rings that my sisters wore
came the tender golden flowers.
I watched them grow from gold to green;
then nuts as large as Tata's head.
I craved the milk I knew they bore.
I listened to the whispering leaves:
to the chattering, rattling, whispering leaves:
when night winds did wake.
They haunt me still in work and play:
those whispering leaves behind the slit
on the cabin wall of childhood's
dreaming and becoming.

Dusk in Africa

Lizzie Ngwenya
Swaziland, b. 1971

The cattle are brought in from grazing,
birds stop singing in the forest,
the last buckets of water are brought in,
a little light is seen from each hut.

Women have gathered their young around the fire,
protecting them from the spirit of dark
which is said to be awaking
when the sun goes to sleep.
Every mouth is fed with fufu and groundnut soup.

The silence is broken by the chirping of a cricket.
The full moon is out, to greet the night,
the bats flutter about in the moonlight.

Day is done.
Gone the sun.
It's dusk in Africa . . .

My Home That Would Never Exist

Michael Powell
South Africa, b. 1955

This place is a quiet place,
With gardens and valleys,
And woods of pine trees,
But it's far from home.

There's no killing or fighting,
But just peace and quiet,
And the people are happy,
But it's far from home.

But when I think of this place at night,
How I wish it could exist,
So that there would be peace and quiet,
But this place would be far from home.

At Play

Catching a Porcupine

Stephen Watson
South Africa, b. 1954

Father used to say
if I were out hunting,
having to sit waiting,
waiting for a porcupine,
the time is always best
when the Milky Way turns back –
this is the time
when a porcupine returns.

Father also said
I should feel the wind.
He used to say
I should be careful
always to taste
the direction of the wind.
The porcupine is not a thing
which will return, he'd say,
coming with the wind.
Rather, it moves
slant-wise, across it,
so that it can better
sniff the air and tell
if danger lurks ahead.

Father used to say
I should breathe softly
when sitting, waiting
for a porcupine.
It is a thing, he said
which hears everything.
I must not even
make a rustling.
I must sit deadstill.

Father taught me
about the stars.
He used to say
that whenever I
was sitting by a burrow,
I should watch the stars,
the places where they fell.
I should, above all,
watch them keenly,
for the places where stars fall,
he often taught,
really are the places
where porcupines can be caught.

Spring Song

Jeni Couzyn
South Africa, b. 1942

spring is come
the world is begun
Spring is come
the World is begun
come out
come out
the world is begun

blue is begun
the sky is out
flesh feet air is out
laughter is out
come out come out
spring is come
green is out
the world is Begun

sun is out
the world is begun
spring is COME

come to me come
out of the darkness
into the brightness
come
out of darkness
spring
into the brightness
spring is come
is come
the world is begun
love is out

love is begun
light is out
the world is begun
Spring is come
the World is begun
the world is
Begun.

Pear

Ruth Jacobson
South Africa

Like a golden
    sun-drop
Caught in
    mid-plop
By the leafy arm
Of a care-free
    pear-tree
Ready to
Let go, and
    drop.

Song of a Stick Fighter

Motshile wa Nthodi
South Africa, b. 1948

O ... we ... e ...
be a man
and show your skill.

I'll beat you once
on the knee,
twice on your right
side ribs,
up I cross your belly
touch your chin,
down shaving your
hair with a blow
of no return.

Ha ...
be a man,
come on.
come on − *woza*!
show your skill.

Ewe − ewe − ewe ...

Going Up Going Down

*Nibor Nalam
South Africa, b. 1940*

In the big city
In the shopping malls
High tall buildings
Father calls them skyscrapers
We're off to play the lifts
First get past the security guards

Duck and dive and slither past!
The ones I like best
are the fish-bowl ones
that slide up and down on the outside
You can see everyone
and everyone can see you
Security guards too
But they can't catch you
Because up you shoot
Fast!
      opsh!
    o
     o
      o
     o
    o

Who   Wait, first get my
Where's my stomach gone?
Then push Ground again and   S   a
Ker   c   H   T
   d   o   m
  o
   o   back
    o
    o   h   c   a
    oink!   S   T   O   M
Stomach's down in my boots
Let's go and try another one   in its

                  S   O   A   h
                    T   m   c

                  usual

              s t o m a c h

                  place.

Me (or Soccer in the Street)

Mark Finkenstein
South Africa, b. 1952

wearing colours
white, black white

two towers
on the side

under me, a
green brilliance

right half
covering up

left half
passes

crowd screaming
mad

me racing down   inside right   inside left and left wing
the wing   juggling the ball

centre forward just
received it

nearer now, we   defence rattled   I hear a thud!
dash forward   get the head to it   the net shudders

GOAL!!

a car hoots
We
All
Scatter!

The Wind

Said Farah
Somalia, b. 1972

a small boy of five talking to his friends

There ... can you see him?
... There he goes!
He sure is fast, isn't he?
I know you feel him.
But tell me ...
Can you see my friend the wind?
He's strong, you know ...
Stronger than me, stronger than a tractor
even!
He can knock down buildings,
and I've heard that he even kills people.
But he's nice to me ...
my friend the wind.
Can you see my friend the wind?
... You want to know a secret?
... I CAN!

Upside-Down Cake

I Choonara
South Africa

I am going to make
An upside-down cake.
I know I'll need some flour,
But I'm going to wait
At least half an hour
Before I begin to bake.

I'll need some fat
And eggs, and water,
Sugar in an upside-down bowl
And mix all of that.

Before I can really begin
I'll need an upside-down tin,
And an upside-down oven
To fit everything in.

I know you will say
I will have to stand on my head
To eat an upside-down cake.
But I have thought of that:
I will choke and be dead.

So I will change my mind
And bake instead
A sideways cake
And eat it
Sideways in bed.

Fable

Jose Craveirinha
Mozambique, b. 1922

Fat boy bought a balloon
and blew
he blew the yellow balloon with much strength.

Fat boy blew
blew
blew
the balloon filled up
filled up
and burst open!

Thin boys picked up the scraps
and made small balloons.

The 800 Metres

Roderick Baard
South Africa, b. 1953

Bang!
There goes the gun
Up goes Gaston
As expected
Here come I
As expected.
Panting behind me
Keith!
First bend
Keith ahead
No pain in legs
Feeling fit,
Feeling fine.
Gaston!
Gaston!
Crowd going wild
Hah
I'll show them
Here I go
Sprinting ahead.
Crowd going wild
Gaston!
Baard!
Heh Heh!
Keith ahead
Again!
Gaston striding well,
Pant Pant
Rubber in my legs
Pain in chest
In legs
In Ego
Damn!
Jose pulling hard

Passes
John feeling well
Passes
Blood in head
No legs left
No life left
Gaston!
Gaston!
Crowd going
Wild.
Hah!
A sweet smell of grass,
A sweet, sweet smell of grass,
Coaxing my cheek
A tap on the shoulder
"What happened, Rod?"
A silly, tired smile:
"Bad start."

Bang!
There goes the gun
David up.
Crowd going wild
Pain in chest (in legs, in ego)
Bad Start?

The Goey-Gumdy

Michael Kuus
South Africa, b. 1954

The day was horch,
And I was on a hunt
Riding my faithful glugy-glog.

And there before me was a goey-gumdy,
Not one but two goey-gumdys.
It was a spill as I sat frivering.

The slelly-like hands reached forward,
But my glugy-glog gote it down,
Because it was his favourite flavour, "Strawberry".

But with a slunt the other goey-gumdy
Slurped up my glugy-glog.

I pulled out my frun,
And zeeshed the other one.
The goey-gumdy melted,
And out joped my glugy-glog.
We lived a hinted life for ever after!

The High Jump

Colin Muskett
South Africa, b. 1953

The huge crowd, a glittering panorama
of faces, waiting.
Expectancy in the air.
In the middle of the stadium, I stand,
a small figure fidgeting in the sun.

Moist hands clammy at my side,
the sun burning my neck.
A shimmering heat haze sears my eyes.

The bar is in position.

A stuffy silence washes over the crowd
like a hot wave.
I feel eyes on me.
It seems physically impossible
to start that run-up,
like something cold and brittle inside
would break like gut.
My legs are leaden heavy.
But then, I shake myself,
Cough,
look around,
breathe deeply,
and leaning forward, mesmerised by the bar,
I
    run
        forward.

Suspended for that split second I
feel horizontal, weightless, conscious
of the deep blue of the sky.
And then,
with shouts in my ears,
I land,
in an ungainly heap
on the
other
side.

Moon a Balloon

Essop Patel
South Africa, b. 1930

for Muhammed Farouk Rasheed Ahmed & Molseen

the moon
        drifting
            across
                the sky ...

            a child
                tugging
                    on
                        a piece
                            of string ...

                    a balloon
                        moving
                            between
                                the clouds ...

Children's Rain Song

Musaemura Zimunya
Zimbabwe, b. 1940

I see little children
fling their small clothes away
like merry flying termites
after their rainy wedding flights
skipping, hopping and screaming in the rain

Rain fall fall
we will eat berries
rain fall for all
we will eat mealies
we will eat cucumbers
rain fall fall

Little brown bodies
shrieking in the rain
laughing and playing
splattering in the puddles
loving all the rain

Rain fall fall
we will eat berries
Ambuya's groundnuts
Mother's groundnuts
we will eat all

Children in the rain
they don't feel the pain
of longing all the time
to streak through my years
and dance in the rain again.

On Holiday

Louise Eyeington
Swaziland, b. 1968

Bodies
Grilling
Sizzling
In their oily coverings
Lie like sardines
Sunbathing

Large ladies
Bulging out of frilly swimsuits
Like blobs of white bread dough
They float
Face up
Their puckered buttocks, spilling out,
Are hidden –
For a while

Young boys
Strut
Creating
A parade, a show, a market,
Girls giggle, flutter
Others laugh, wide mouthed

Umbrellas
Bikinied bodies
Seaweed
Sunburn
People, everywhere people
All pretending
All "on holiday"

My Family

Kariuki

Joseph Gatuiria
Kenya

The hour of midnight met with a gathering of mothers,
Their only talk … names upon names.
   "It will be my nephew," one said,
   "No, my sister's cousin."
   "Kirahiu is the name or should it be Mwangi?"
Then I heard the delicate squeal of a baby
(It is of an hour's age)
   Caused no less than a whole village to awake.
   What causes them to awake?
   And an old man comes struggling into the house.

"How are you, Kariuki?" This he whispers
To the deaf stranger of this world.
   Whereupon the "Kariuki" begins its endless journey.
   It floats from mouth to mouth.
   "It's a boy! Kariuki is born."
   The old warrior is born again.

from Not Him

Wopko Jensma
South Africa, b. 1939

he forbids us to dance
he always leads the church service
he has a stable job
he is always on time for work
he never gets drunk
he has respect for most people
everybody respects him
we love our daddy
but sometimes i notice
when a kwela blasts from the radio
he wiggles his toes

A Conversation with My Son

Dikobe wa Mogale
South Africa, b. 1957

Johannesburg Prison, April 30 1988

taking me by the hand
and pulling me towards
the visitors' exit door
my six-year-old son said
       come home with us now daddy

i cannot said i
because i am a political prisoner
and must stay here for some time
     then i will stay here with you
     he replied emphatically

no mandela i replied gently
you cannot stay here
with your daddy
only political prisoners
stay here and –
     daddy! he interjected excitedly
     with sweet innocence
     daddy then tell them
     i am also a political prisoner ...

Brown Lullaby

Adam Small
South Africa, b.1936

They call your mama girl
love
they call your mama girl
all places that she go
they call your mama girl
they see to all the white man first
your mama she must wait
your mama she must wait very long
afore they call her girl
but your mama she come home
love
your mama she come home
for nothin' but to love you
your mama she come home
an' she love you more than she got to wait
aye even more
an' more today than yesterday
more every day

Ask Grandpa

Musaemura Zimunya
Zimbabwe, b. 1949

Ask Grandpa
he will tell you
he will educate you
ask him
ask him

who knows
why buses are
moving coffins
he knows
ask him
ask him

who knows
how the last lion
hid in a woman's womb
and came out
in the form of a man
he knows
ask him
ask him

who knows
why cities are jungles
too tough for you
he knows
ask him
listen and ponder

My Grandmother is My Love

Eric Mazani
Zimbabwe, b. 1948

I love my grandmother with the whole of my heart.
Now she is an old, ancient girl her face has changed, of course.
My grandmother of ninety years is my love.
She is a teller of tales.
She is old, bold and always cold.
Indeed, she is never far from a fire-place.
'Makadzoka' she is called, for she once died.
After some time she rose from death.
'Mushakabvudimbu' they call her in Shona – half-dead.
My life is in her hands and the life of my family too.
She is a half witch, having been taught to cure with herbs.
Little, thin grandmother of mine!
Looking so young because of eating so many sweets!
Sugar-sucker! Ten teaspoons full in each cup of tea!
My old ambuya! Makadzoka is my goddess.
She hates dirt, noise, quarrels and dry food.
She is ever sitting on her mat in the sun
Or otherwise hunting for herbs.
She is ever smiling, but an egg grows in her mouth when
One annoys her.
"I wish to die and rest," she says. "When will this world end?
I am tired."

Beside her is a packet of sugar, a sweet sauce of peppered
    corn.
Her teeth are brown with rust; her nose is sooty with black
    snuff.

Makadzoka is my love. I shall look into her dimples
The laughing dimples are on her chin. They were supposed to
    be
Two but there are now a hundred! There are holes where stag-
    nant water
Was scooped out.

Lovely Mushakabvu
My grandmother
Is my love.

Emerald Dove

Anthony Delius
South Africa, 1916-89

The Xhosa say
When the emerald dove
Sits sobbing in the bush
She is thinking of the terrible wars
And she cries
My father is dead
My mother is dead
My sisters are dead
My brothers are all dead
And my heart goes
Doem Doem
Doem doem doem doem
doem
doem.

Dotito is Our Brother

Charles Mungoshi
Zimbabwe, b. 1947

Dotito is our brother.
He is strange.
He will not play with us on the streets.
He doesn't want to go with us to the Community Centre.
He doesn't want to play the hoola hoop.
He likes sitting under the mango tree
all day long all alone drawing strange things
that look like people but aren't really people
on any scrap of paper. He is at the bottom
of his class and he disappears each time
we go for games in the playground.
He loves the rain. He could walk for hours
in a heavy downpour and never notice.
Father caned him for it once and now when
it rains he just sits by the window looking out;
sometimes talking - opening his mouth
and saying strange noises to the rain.
When he is tired of talking to the rain
he blows breath onto the glass pane
and draws the same weird things as on the scraps of paper.
People who don't know him think he's deaf –
but he isn't although we aren't sure he won't be – soon.
Behind a closed door in their bedroom father and mother
whisper about him in the dark.
Although we aren't supposed to hear it
we know what they have begun to think
about Dotito. We are a little afraid.
Strange people point and stare at us in the street
even when Dotito isn't with us. We know what they
are saying too even when we don't see them open their
   mouths.
We can't go anywhere without meeting them.
They are talking about how we are Dotito's people.

The Sound of the Stars

Stephen Watson from the /Xam
South Africa, b. 1954

When I slept at my grandfather's, in his hut,
I would sit with him, outside in the cool.
I would ask him about the sound which I heard,
which I sometimes seemed to hear speaking.
He'd say it was stars that were speaking.
"The stars say Tsau! They say Tsau! Tsau!"
They are cursing the springbok's eyes, he'd say.
"This is the sound that stars like to make;
and summer's the time they like to sound."

When at my grandfather's, I listened to stars.
I could hear the sound, the speech of the stars.
Tsatsi would say it was these that I heard,
that they were cursing the springboks' eyes
to help us in hunting, in tracking down game.
Later, when full-grown, and a hunter as well,
I was the one who listened, still listened.
I could sit there and hear it come very close:
the star-sound Tsau, sounding Tsau! Tsau!

She Brought Home Poppies

Karen Press
South Africa, b. 1956

she brought home poppies
instead of bread, twelve little suns

the eldest child asked why? why poppies,
buying poppies when there is no food?

she said, look at them, who can be hungry with these
yellow, white, orange suns facing every corner

all night they rustled on their long stems
as if the room were á forest

and the children crying,
she made them into birds in the forest

in the morning the petals had fallen,
pollen dusting the floor, the youngest asked

what will we eat today? collecting the petals
she stored them away carefully

Innocence

Cathy Bell
South Africa

Yesterday I was small
I did not understand
they said it was a funeral
but would there be a band?
cook was crying −
probably broke a plate
granny kissed me
said she was sorry −
for the kiss?
why should I worry?
nanny gave me some flowers
said they were for mother
anyway
where was my mother?
Today I know.

To a Sleeping Child

Shirley Futeran
South Africa, 1954-71

Where were you
little brother
that you didn't feel
my lips on your cheek
and the soft dark weight
of my hair on your face?
Where were you
little scrap
of the flesh that bore me
with the soft heavy beat
of my blood in your veins?

Gone behind the darkness
of the darkness behind,
locked in the blackness
of the blackness inside
the capsule of yourself,
little brother.

Thoughts on Holidays Spent with an Absent Father

Paddi Clay
South Africa, b. 1954

        Memories of a wooden swing
    under a green, amazon tree
        in a strange lush country
Memories
        of a father
                watching
    memories stored in faded photographs
        and empty luggage
                in the cupboard.

Streamside Exchange

John Pepper Clark-Bekederemo
Nigeria, b. 1935

CHILD   River bird, river bird,
        Sitting all day long
        On hook over grass,
        River bird, river bird,
        Sing to me a song
        Of all that pass
        And say,
        Will mother come back today?

BIRD   You cannot know
        And should not bother;
        Tide and market come and go
        And so has your mother.

57

There is no Fixed Time
for Breast-Feeding

Okot p'Bitek
Uganda, b. 1931

from *Song of Lawino*

My husband is angry
Because, he says,
I cannot keep time
And I do not know
How to count the years;

He asks me
How many days
There are in a year,
And how many weeks
In four moons;
But I cannot answer:
The number of moons
In nine weeks
I cannot say!
How can I tell?

Ocol has brought home
A large clock
It goes tock-tock-tock-tock
And it rings a bell.

He winds it first
And then it goes!
But I have never touched it.
I am afraid of winding it!

I wonder what causes
The noise inside it!
And what makes it go!

On the face of the clock
There are writings
And its large single testicle
Dangles below.
It goes this way and that way
Like a sausage-fruit
In a windy storm.

I do not know
How to tell the time
Because I cannot read
The figures.
To me the clock
Is a great source of pride
It is beautiful to see
And when visitors come
They are highly impressed!

And Ocol has strange ways
Of saying what the time is.
In the morning
When the sun is sweet to bask in
He says
"It is Eight o'clock!"
When the cock crows
For the first time
He says
"It is Five!"
Towards the middle of the night,
When wizards are getting ready,
Ocol says
"It is Eleven!"
And after sunset
"It is Seven."

My head gets puzzled,
Things look upside-down

As if I have been
Turning round and round
And I am dizzy.

* * *

My husband says
I am useless
Because I waste time,
He quarrels
Because, he says,
I am never punctual.
He says
He has no time to waste.
He tells me
Time is money.

Ocol does not chat
With me,
He never jokes
With anybody,
He says
He has no time
To sit around the evening fire.

When my husband
Is reading a new book
Or when he is
Sitting in his sofa,
His face covered up
Completely with the big newspaper
So that he looks
Like a corpse,
Like a lone corpse
In the tomb,

He is so silent!
His mouth begins

To decay!

✳ ✳ ✳

I do not know
How to keep the white man's time.
My mother taught me
The way of the Acoli
And nobody should
Shout at me
Because I know
The customs of our people!
When the baby cries
Let him suck milk
From the breast.
There is no fixed time
For breast-feeding.

When the baby cries
It may be he is ill;
The first medicine for a child
Is the breast.
Give him milk
And he will stop crying,
And if he is ill
Let him suck the breast
While the medicine-man
Is being called
From the beer-party.

Children in our homestead
Do not sleep at fixed times:
When sleep comes
Into their head
They sleep,
When sleep leaves their head
They wake up.

When a child is dirty
Give him a wash,
You do not first look at the sun!
When there is no water
In the house
You cannot wash the child
Even if it is time
For his bath!
Listen
My husband,
In the wisdom of the Acoli
Time is not stupidly split up
Into seconds and minutes,
It does not flow
Like beer in a pot
That is sucked
Until it is finished.

It does not resemble
A loaf of millet bread
Surrounded by hungry youths
From a hunt;
It does not get finished
Like vegetables in the dish.

A lazy youth is rebuked,
A lazy girl is slapped,
A lazy wife is beaten,
A lazy man is laughed at
Not because they waste time
But because they only destroy
And do not produce.

from Song of Ocol

Okot p'Bitek
Uganda, b. 1931

Woman,
Shut up!
Pack your things
Go!

Take all the clothes
I bought you
The beads, necklaces
And the remains
Of the utensils,
I need no second-hand things.

There is a large sack
In the boot
Of the car,
Take it
Put all your things in it
And go!

   ✳ ✳ ✳

Houseboy,
Listen
Call the *ayah*
Help the woman
Pack her things,
Then sweep the house clean
And wash the floor,
I am off to Town
To fetch the painter.

Other People

Beachcombing

Peter E Clarke
South Africa, b. 1926

Strolling on the littered beach
his was the eye that would search
for retrievable things,
above the tidal reach,
appealing to curiosity, childish ideas and taste.
Collecting flotsam on the way,
thinking aloud, occasionally he'd say to us,
"I'll take this and this . . . and that . . ."
He'd pick up driftwood to carve
or knock together.

Often he'd find a need for every piece,
fishbone, feather, plant and weed.
"It needn't go to waste."
He'd pick up bits of metal and later
flatten folds and creases
then cut and purposefully
put together different pieces
with carefully placed nails
and lengths of measured wire and wood.
So inventive,
able to improvise easily
he received his buddies' admiration.
It was good to see
the ingenious way his mind functioned
and the slender hands give shape
to things.

Had later times been right,
would that he had tried
to reach the sky.

I Watched Him

Robert van der Valk
South Africa, b. 1951

i watched him.
he moved so slowly,
undisturbed.
he watched the doves
feeding.
he moved so quietly
  silently,
(like a cat).

he turned
and saw me watching,
he stared at me
(through the fence).

then he turned,
(almost casually)
and sauntered off.

the doves departed.

The Sweet Brew at Chitakale

Jack Mapanje
Malawi, b. 1944

The old woman squats before a clay jar of *thobwa*
She uncovers the basket lid from the jar and
Stirs attention with a gourdful of the brew.

The customers have all been here: cyclists
In dripping sweat have deposited their coins
In the basket, gulping down their share.

Pedestrians on various chores have talked
Before the exchange and then cooled their
Parched throats to their money's worth,

But this bus passenger bellows for a gourdful
From the window, drinks deliberately slowly until
The conductor presses the go-button −

The woman picks up the pieces of her broken
Gourd, and dusting her bottom, again squats
Confronting her brew with a borrowed cup.

No Letters − Yet

Pip Broadbent
South Africa

Harry − not one word and thirty-four days.
Perhaps nothing more.
But I had not realized that for you
it would be so difficult
to put pen to paper.
Please don't
if it all meant nothing.

Harry, are you enjoying not writing?
Are you enjoying knowing
that I am waiting?
Are you enjoying forgetting?

Or − are you writing?

The Sprinter

Jared Angira
Kenya

I heard your voice
echo
through the reeds

I saw your shadow
float
on the water

I felt your scent
come
through the wind

I saw your image
in the dream

I saw you run on boulder rocks
and laugh
with cattle egrets
and kiss the osaye fruits
and I sprinted
but where were you to be trapped?

Jonice

Atukwei Okai
Ghana, b. 1941

Sleep
    not
        on the sleeping
Wall –
    come sleep
On my
    shoulder;
        why do
You
    prefer
The wall
    to my human
Shoulder? it
May be coldly
        tall, but
I am
    near
And fonder;
    I have sent
You
    the call,
        wishing to
Be
    the sole
Holder
    of the head
        that
Will fall
    from
Your neck
    whose moulder
        has
Given
    me

You -
    and all
                for now till
When
    we grow
Older;
    sleep not
                on the
Sleeping wall -
Come sleep on my shoulder.

Happy Little Boy

Robert van der Valk
South Africa, b. 1951

happy little boy,
(so far away)
swings in a perfect light.
in a land
(of toffee)
where little boys
(and little girls)
can play.
in a land
there isn't night

or day.

Pedestrian, to Passing Benz-Man

Albert Ojuka
Kenya

You man, lifted gently
out of the poverty and suffering
we so recently shared; I say –
why splash the muddy puddle on to
my bare legs, as if, still unsatisfied
with your seated opulence
you must sully the unwashed
with your diesel-smoke and mud-water
and force him buy, beyond his means,
a bar of soap from your shop?
a few years back we shared a master
today you have none, while I have
exchanged a parasite for something worse.
But maybe a few years is too long a time.

One for the Road

Charles Mungoshi
Zimbabwe, b. 1947

He came in
dusty sweaty red-rimmed eyes
ordered a Coke, downed it in one gulp,
picked up his bag with a woman's clothing in it
slung it over hunched shoulders
and turned to go –
It was then we noticed
the black band pinned on his coat sleeve ...

72

The Untold Dream

Ayanda Madide
South Africa

She dances to music nobody else can hear,
She exists in a world of her own;
where everything is ruled by fear;
where the wind sings sad songs every day;
where the days are as dark as the nights;
Her life is a dream she can never tell to anybody.

An Epitaph

Julius Chingono
Zimbabwe, b. 1949

Here lies Stephen Pwanya
A renowned gentleman
who lived to forty-five
he is survived by his pipe
the smoke could not wait
took to the wind.

Little Girl

Jeremy Gordin
South Africa, b. 1952

In slanted
Autumn sun
(leaves ruffling
on moist
red earth)

little girl
(dirty-faced
blonde-haired)
hides in a bush
(a world
her own).

Little girl
is worth
one million
works of art

perhaps more.

Old Age

Mteto Mzongwana
South Africa, b. 1957

Early morning
the bell rings.
It is a quarter to seven,
the time
that I always walk
past the barbed-wire fence.
Some are awake,
washing their eyes
in the concrete sink.
They walk around
like old apes
locked in a zoo cage –
others are sitting
on these lonely pieces
of wood
watching little children
playing games
they used to play when they were young.

They are tired
of going on a dreadful journey,
and think that life
is short for them.
Maybe it is – but nobody knows.

Peak Hour

Michele Freind
South Africa, b. 1952

see all the funnylittlepeople
where they going to?
don't know.
you know?

                              no.

they know?

                              no.

they stream from the station
       stream
they stream across the roads
       stream

they waste theirfunnylittlelives
in
dull dingy
grey grimy
sunless stinky
funnylittleboxes
      offices.

little do they know
that
when
            they die
they'll still stay
in
dull dingy
grey grimy
sunless stinky
notsofunnylittleboxes
      coffins.

Elsie

Bernard Levinson
South Africa, b. 1926

Elsie talked to God from her flat in Hillbrow.
Perched on the edge of her bath
she discussed the price of bread
and the things the butcher said
when she couldn't decide.

She was always grateful that He found her.
Between the Swop-shop and the Coffee bar
one could miss the door –
the metal steps to the fourth floor
and the dark corner
where the refuse drain rumbled and coughed.

The sun falls amongst chimneys
splinters in a million windows –
Are you there Elsie?
Are you there in the darkness –
in your own secret care
holding the remains of the day in a shopping bag?
Are you talking to God?

Hey, Beggar

Shelley Swade
South Africa, b. 1952

Hey, beggar,
Old tattered man,
Sing with the wolves
To the moon
And the grain.

Laugh, old beggar,
With the wind
In your cheek
And the sound
Of the sea
In your shell.

Cold, beggar,
Freeze with the tree
In the snow,
Fringe your beard
With the frost
Of your bed.

And hey, beggar,
With the sun
In your eye
And a tooth
In the earth.

Sandy beggar,
Heaving the hay,
Be buried
With your body
Whole.

Jacobus

Robert Dederick
South Africa, 1919-83

A thousand miles a year or more
Jacobus travels from floor to floor,
Sighing through his vertical day,
Defeating gravity either way;
Descending only – it is plain –
In order to ascend again,
He falls to the level of the street,
To cars, No-Parking signs, and feet
Only in order to rise once more
To the 8th, 9th or 13th floor,
The lodging ledge the white gull seeks,
The shriek the mad South Easter shrieks.
"Going up," "Going down," Jacobus will call,
But in fact he is going nowhere at all:
However he plunges, however he soars,
Jacobus is caught between two floors.

The Graceful Giraffe Cannot Become a Monkey

Okot p'Bitek
Uganda, b. 1931

from *Song of Lawino*

My husband tells me
I have no ideas
Of modern beauty.
He says
I have stuck
To old-fashioned hair-styles.
He says
I am stupid and very backward,
That my hair-style
Makes him sick
Because I am dirty.

It is true
I cannot do my hair
As white women do.

Listen,
My father comes from Payira,
My mother is a woman of Koc!
I am a true Acoli
I am not a half-caste
I am not a slave-girl;
My father was not brought home
By the spear
My mother was not exchanged
For a basket of millet.

Ask me what beauty is
To the Acoli
And I will tell you;
I will show it to you

If you give me a chance!

You once saw me,
You saw my hair-style
And you admired it,
And the boys loved it.
At the arena
Boys surrounded me
And fought for me.

My mother taught me
Acoli hair fashions;
Which fits the kind
Of hair of the Acoli,
And the occasion.

Listen,
Ostrich plumes differ
From chicken feathers,
A monkey's tail
Is different from that of the giraffe,
The crocodile's skin
Is not like the guinea fowl's,
And the hippo is naked, and hairless.

Pioneer Street is Dying

Charles Mungoshi
Zimbabwe, b. 1947

Pioneer Street is dying.
Only a few of the old buildings still
stand like the serrated teeth of old men.

Slowly an old man gropes
his way through the rubble.
The cruel wind pinches his eyes.

He stops in the lee
of some old wall out of the wind
surveying his yesterdays –

then quickly, on seeing me, hurries on
fingering the wilted rose
stuck in his button-hole.

Young Shepherd Bathing His Feet

Peter E Clarke
South Africa, b. 1926

Only the short, broad, splayed feet
Moved ...

Feet that had trodden over
Soft soil,
Sand,
Ploughed veld,
Mountain rocks
And along narrow tracks,
On Winter clay and
Dust of
Summer roads ...

The short, broad, splayed feet
Moved
In and Out ...

The stumpy toes stretched wide
Apart
And closed together
Then opened wide ...

In ecstasy.

Ali the Driver

Martin Brennan
Nigeria

Ali the Driver at the wheel
Bare is his foot from toe to heel
Ali the Driver big and fat
With a moon-round face and a Muslim's hat.

Ali the Driver with a big white grin
See how he crashes the gears in.
Ali the Driver in his car
Bumps over laterite, stone and tar.

Ali the Driver mechanical king
Can deal with practically everything,
Punctures, breakdowns and tanks that leak,
Brakes and rods and springs that squeak.

Ali the Driver at the wheel
Bare is his foot from toe to heel.
Ali the Driver big and fat
With a moon-round face and a Muslim's hat.

Tribute to a Boy

Michael Strauss
South Africa

It had been a hard day.
Up and down the toiling busy streets –
The heat of the day –
The growl of the engine –
The incessant noise of the bell.
He moved his clammy hands on the wheel.

A small boy
Returning from an afternoon in town,
Clambered onto this vehicle of adventure
And hurried up the aisle to meet the driver.

"Hi!"
The driver turned round, a scowl on his weary face.
He saw the young face turned up to him
The eager eyes sparkling with excitement,
And a smile crept over his face.
"Hi!"

Two Men and the Axe

S Lubega
Uganda, b. 1945

Two men were walking along a road
When one man saw an axe.
"Look, what a fine axe,"
Said one to the other.
"Let us take it away
And sell it," said the other.
"But it's my axe,
I found it," said the first.
"Is it your axe?
I thought it ours,
Not just yours or mine."
"You're just saying that.
I tell you it's mine."
"O.K. very well. It's yours."
About twenty minutes later
Came a man running.
"Look, he's calling us,"
Said the first to the second.
"Then let us wait and listen."
"Stop! Stop! I say."
"What do you want?"
"I want my axe," said the third.
"Do you hear?
He wants his axe back."
"Yes, you have taken it,
And it was not yours."
"I did not take it," said the second,
"It was my friend here."
"What do you mean?" retorted the first,
"We both took it."
But the second replied,
"When we took the axe,
It was *yours* not ours."

Two Worlds

Thabang Thoka
South Africa, b. 1963

How is it that you have
and I don't have
that you can
and I can't?

How is it that you will
and I won't
that you shall
and I shall not?

How is it that you have
and I haven't
that you receive
yet I don't?

How is it that you laugh
and I cry
that you eat
and I starve?

How is it that you are
and I'm not
that you live
yet I die?

How is it that our worlds are so different
and yet so close?

My Shoes

Taziona Chaponda
Malawi, b. 1974

I bought this really nice pair of shoes,
They were R200,
They'll really improve my running.

Our maid receives R80 for her month's pay,
Her son needs R50 school fees,
And she needs R150 to feed the family.
I'm not going to wear my shoes.

Emily

Esther van der Vyver
South Africa

I know a little bird of a woman
Who wheezes my welcome
and extends her cluster of
little white bones
which I hold in my hand
like a secret.

Away from the Rain

Ronald H Louw
South Africa

We tuck our newspapers
Under our raincoats
Away from the rain
As we run to our cars,
While others tuck in their babes
Under their breasts
Away from the rain
That runs in their houses.

Eternity

Jennifer Venter
South Africa

The bus stopped
at the
    bus-stop –
gobbled up the worm of people
and moved on
    and on
        and

Traffic Jam

J O Ige
Sierra Leone

The man in the Mercedes
Sleeps with his head on the steering
While the man on the bicycle flies past.

A Little Man

Susan Latimer
South Africa

That little man over there
with his briefcase
(full of the *most important* documents)
and his neat shirt, button-down collar,
dustless shoes and immaculate suit
is looking up at the sky
for the first time in his life
tonight –
and he's annoyed,
because the moon
(in its third waning day)
is not perfectly
round.

Places

HOLIDAY

©1983 JOHN N. MUAFANGEJO.

The Name of My Place

Stephen Watson from the /Xam
South Africa, b. 1954

You have not heard,
I have not told how I,
a convict at that time,
first went travelling in a train,
how I would have fallen out
had not a woman dragged me back,
and how nice it was to sit in it,
the two of us then seated there:
I and one black man.

You have not heard,
nor have I yet said
how his face was black,
how this black man's mouth
was also black;
how the white men are those
whose faces are red,
they being to me
the handsome men.

You have not heard
and I have not yet said
how it was this black man
who asked me then:
"What is your place, its name?"
How I replied, "I come
from that place, called home."
How he asked again,
"Tell me, what is its name?"
And how I, called //Kabbo, said:

"My place is Bitterpits."

Cape Flats

Karen Press
South Africa, b. 1956

old washing strung out:
  wind and sand beat, relentless,
at rows of tired eyes

Ibadan

John Pepper Clark-Bekederemo
Nigeria, b. 1935

Ibadan,
  running splash of rust
and gold – flung and scattered
among seven hills like broken
china in the sun.

My Old Shoe

Julius Chingono
Zimbabwe, b. 1949

Makes little sounds
clop, clop, clop.
grins broadly
reveals dirty teeth
five in number
embedded in its jaws
like a swimming fish
as I haunt the sunny streets.

Windy Morning

Jessica Abrahams
South Africa, b. 1957

The sun climbs steadily over
the long long hill casting a
golden cloak over the frosted grass.
He teases my eyelids open and
I wake to see the neighbours'
blanket blowing in the wind.
Pink, like my pet rabbit's nose,
it snuffles, wuffles as if chewing
a tasty carrot.
The grass caresses the earth
with silvery waves and ripples,
and I think of the seagulls,
screaming as they drift
on the tide of the wind.

Joy

Stuart Stromin
South Africa

hitch-hiking
sixty miles on a map.
country to city
scenery pretty.

and you may ask me, "How's life?"
and i'll tell you that i saw a field of happy sunflowers, free,
looking at the sun,
except for one,
which was smiling at me.

Nothing There!

Nibor Nalam
South Africa, b.1940

Oogh! Grunch!

Leap – Hah!

I'll bet that's happened to you
You're going along just fine
Not a care in the world
When suddenly you
                    step on the stair
that isn't
            there

Shantytown

Anonymous

High on the veld upon that plain
And far from streets and lights and cars
And bare of trees, and bare of grass,
Jabavu sleeps beneath the stars.

Jabavu sleeps.
The children cough.
Cold creeps up, the hard night cold,
The earth is tight within its grasp,
The highveld cold without soft rain,
Dry as the sand, rough as a rasp,
The frost-rimmed night invades the shacks.
Through dusty ground
Through rocky ground
Through freezing ground the night cold creeps.
In cotton blankets, rags and sacks
Beneath the stars Jabavu sleeps.

One day Jabavu will awake
To greet a new and shining day:
The sounds of coughing will become
The children's laughter as they play
In parks with flowers where dust now swirls
In strong-walled homes with warmth and light.
But for tonight Jabavu sleeps.
Jabavu sleeps. The stars are bright.

Stones, Sky, Radio

Ingrid de Kok
South Africa, b. 1951

Around the roots of the tree
the children are dicing with stones.
The sky is immense as the sky,
the sun is as hot as the noonday sun,
the red ants are industrious as ants.
The children are dicing with stones.

Across the grey veld a man is walking.
He is neither young nor old.
He is holding a stick and kicking a tin
and walks like a man walking
across the veld in the dust.

In the distance a radio crackles
out of a cluster of huts.
This is not a sign of life.
It is a radio in the village.

There is nothing else to see or hear
at this time and place, apparently.
The children are still dicing with stones.

Exiled Farmer

Chenjerai Hove
Zimbabwe, b.1954

Don't close the window
Or curtain it,
For Africa speaks outside:
The splatter of raindrops on the heart
Sings eternal songs:
Would my drummer were here.

Wild Mushroom

Shimmer Chinodya
Zimbabwe, b. 1957

Here are umbrellas pitched this sunny afternoon
On a sea-less infinite beach of grass,
　　Scrubs and rocks
　　Red, brown
　　White, yellow
　　Even black! fleshy umbrellas
　　of various sizes. Pitched.
　　In brilliant clusters
　　Giving shade to no one.

I expected sun-bathing midgets under
　　Such umbrellas, but
　　Seeing there is no one around and
　　Even for the tiniest midget
　　We may as well do some picking;
　　We will only need careful picking to turn
　　These fleshy umbrellas
　　Into tasty relish.

What They Say about Pickles

Masautso Chaponda
Malawi, b. 1971

They asked. "Zimbabwe!" said I.
They asked. "Oh ... just to buy some pickles."
What was that?
"I said just to buy a bottle of pickles."
What is that?
"Vegetables in brine."
See, they don't have pickles in Zambia
so I reckoned I could go across.
Those pickles, I do miss them.
They asked. "I'll be back in a day," I assured.
Passport! "Oh ... here it is"
Currency? "Thirty dollars."
Where from? "Umm ... my mother gave me."
They asked. "I said my mother gave me the money"
Dollars? Your mother? Zambia?
"Why not?" I asked,
"My mother had them all along."
You can't go!
not for pickles! with dollars from your mother!
"Why not?"
It is law.
Going is law? Dollars is law?
Zambia is law? Pickles is law?
My mother-in-law would have given a better excuse.

Things I have seen

Karen Press
South Africa, b. 1956

Bougainvillea on a white wall
Sunlight in the leaves
Two black feet a twisted mouth
Cold shadows blowing through the grass
Red petals fall and rot
A spade opening the earth

Yeoville Park, 1986

Jeremy Gordin
South Africa, b. 1952

The high-
pitched whistle and call
of the mielie-seller
through the dark cold
of a Highveld evening
drawing in, the after-smell
of *slap* chips and vinegar
on my fingers. What's changed
in 16 years is that mother's hot stew
is not waiting nor is dad
walking in from work. But little Jeremy
is still out on the patchy grass,
unhappy, directionless, and up to no good in his head,
now as then.

Ithemba Alibulali: Hope Does Not Kill

Nibor Nalam
South Africa, b. 1940

If you're cold or dying of heat,
I will say without any fuss
There's nothing at all that can beat
A rattletrap African bus.

They're large and they're loud and they're old
And they belch amazing black fumes,
With a driver who's certain to scold
In a voice that bellows and booms.

"Merry Christmas" in tinsel it says
In bright loops that circle his head.
It's June, but nobody cares,
If it's shiny and silver and red.

The best place to meet a new bus
Is riding behind it uphill.
You get really close in, and thus,
When you're standing virtually still,

You can read what it says on the back:
"Say What!" or "Never say die",
"Hope does not kill" or "Do not attack
From Behind" – who would? and just why?

Bus station is noisy and packed
As women sell boiled chicken's feet,
And roasted green mielies are stacked
In piles where several queues meet.

There's vetkoek and avocado pear
And amasi and Fanta and beer,

If there's something you didn't buy there
You can be sure you'll get it right here.

I make my way to the bus route
That passes my family's homestead.
Stray goats and some chickens I scoot
Out of my way: "Watch out or you 're dead!"

The driver and some other men
Stand up on the roof as they stack
Suitcases, baskets, a hen.
They shout and they heave and they pack.

We move in the red dust that lifts.
The driver shouts: "All get inside!"
The key turns, the gear-lever shifts,
And he swings the steering-wheel wide.

With a rumble and then with a thump
Our old bus gets off on its way.
First a tumble and then a big bump
As we all get used to the sway.

I'm standing jam-packed in the aisle,
Not holding, it's such a tight fit.
Umfundisi's reading his Bible,
His stick pokes me right in the rib.

A mother, who's large both aft and fore,
She crowds into me, long and thin.
She holds chickens, heads to the floor,
Their beaks peck away at my shin.

We talk and we laugh and we sleep
As the bus flies along like a bat.
When – doesn't it just make you weep?
"All out, people!" We've got a flat!

So there's much pushing and shoving
And we make a quick party – why not?
It's a real good time that we're having –
Anyway, plenty of time's what we've got

So why moan? Just all lend a hand,
Let's get this show back on the road.
Whoops – now we've got stuck in the sand.
"Out!" and we walk to lighten the load.

In the end we get there. Mother sings
"Uyafika!" and dances for joy
At the food and the presents he brings.
"Uyafika!" Who has arrived? Me, her big boy!

City-bound Train

Ntsieni N Ndou
Zimbabwe

Packed in each coach
As the engine pulls with force
Our relatives leave us
To seek money to feed us.
Like a snake it twines the mountains
With coaches bound like chains:
All the strong brothers, city-bound!

The Shell

Denzil Gunning
South Africa, b. 1951

It lay there in the pool,
Its mother-of-pearl glistened as the water rippled,
And it seemed to retract from my groping hand,
As I stretched out and grasped it.

I pressed it to my ear and listened.
I listened to the roar of the breakers,
And was hypnotized by the decades of sound
That unfurled and vibrated in my ear from this shell.
It told of happy aquatic days,
And I, in understanding,
Threw it out to sea.

The Mist

Mpho Mamashela
Lesotho, b. 1964

Slowly it comes creeping over the
mountains and tree tops.
Like a small boy to a sleeping grasshopper.

Not a leaf shakes nor twig cracks,
As it weaves its way through the surrounding forests.

Like a lazy cat on a sleeping lap,
it settles on the sleeping hill.
To leave in the later hours, quietly
as it came,
Unveiling the new day.

Wind

Michael O'Hara
Zambia, b. 1969

It's a vicious thing, is wind.
It blows bark from trees
soil from fields
hair from your head
and words from your mouth.
It may even blow husband from wife.

Dilemma of a Ghost

Ama Ata Aidoo
Ghana, b. 1942

One early morning,
When the moon was up
Shining as the sun,
I went to Elmina Junction
And there, and there
I saw a wretched ghost
Going up and down
Singing to himself:
  "Shall I go
To Cape Coast,
Or to Elmina?
I don't know,
I can't tell.
I don't know,
I can't tell."

I Wonder

Nomsa Dlamini
Swaziland, b. 1974

I wonder why the grass is green,
why the wind is invisible,
who taught the birds to build
the nests? and also made
the trees to stand still and rest.

Who paints the rainbow in the sky?
and makes the clouds up high?
Who forms all the stars in the sky?
and when the moon is not round,
where can the other piece be found?

Stay You Well

Jessica Abrahams
South Africa, b. 1957

Like a naughty boy
      Sun slid down
the
    polished
          blue
             stair
                rail
                  and
                      fell
      laughing into the sea.
A million splashes of water
    touched the sticky dark sky
and stayed, sparkling

6-hour Time Difference

Nibor Nalam
South Africa, b. 1940

Wrenched from the dead depths of sleep
The dark shattered by the siren-sudden phone
Hand flings out, fumbles, finds
"Yes? Who is it?"
"It's me, Nkosinathi, calling from Canada."
Breath-bereft, voice raw with fright
Why is he phoning in the middle of the night?
"What's the matter, Nathi?"
"I just have to tell you . . ."
"What? What, Nathi?"
"Snow."
"What? . . . didn't catch . . ."
"It's snowing here! I've just been outside
playing in the snow!
It's my first time ever to see snow!
It's great!
And you? How're you?"

The Fair

Gavin Kaplan
South Africa, b. 1956

The Big Wheel goes round
And round.
It brings me only to the place
Where I started.

It was fun being on top
For a while
Looking down
On everybody
Taking their chances
(How many chances has a man?)

I heard the shot that shattered
The heart of a duck
But these hearts are clay
And may be shattered for a
Cigar or a stay-hot tea-pot
(Could a heart be shattered for less?)

"Roll up," the man said, "Roll up
And see the fattest man in the world."
I see the crowd paying at his booth
(Must I, too, grow fat to earn attention?)

With a sudden jerk
And sickening sway
The Big Wheel starts to move
And brings me back again
To where I started.

The Smart Shoe

Candy Neubert
South Africa

I found a shoe beside the road.
It was a smart shoe.
It was blue and red and yellow and green.
It was for a left foot.
I looked for another shoe, but there was only one.

I put it on.
It was big, and it was smart.
I kept it on my foot and walked home.

My friends said: Simphiwe, you have only one shoe.
I said yes, but it is smart.
My sister said: Simphiwe, you have only one shoe, and it is
                        silly.
I said no, it is not; it is smart.

I found my mother.
She said: where did you find that smart shoe?
I found it by the road, I said. It is smart, isn't it?
Yes, it is, she said. But you have only one.
I will make another shoe for my right foot, I said.

I went into the yard.
I saw a blue tin and a red bucket and yellow paper and a
    green skirt on the washing line.
I saw blue sky and red flowers and yellow sand and green
    grass.
Nothing for making shoes.

Mother said: do you think it would be smart to take that shoe
                    back to the road? Maybe someone has lost it.
                    Maybe they will find it and have two shoes again.

I took the shoe back to the road.
The next morning, it was gone.

109

The Only Wish

Muzi Maziya and John Ambrose
Swaziland & Lesotho, b. 1972

a poem by young boys to their peers in the world

The only wish for our South African friends
   is freedom, peace
   and happiness.
For years they have suffered
   injustices, torture
   and death.
The only wish for our Ethiopian friends
   is food, peace
   and happiness.
For years they have suffered
   from famine, starvation
   and disease.
The only wish for our Bolivian friends
   is to be free, free
   from the evil grips of cocaine.
For years they have suffered
   from horrors and adverse effects
   of cocaine.
The only wish for our Afghanistani friends
   is peace, liberty
   and justice.
For years they have suffered
   the consequences of war,
   preventing prosperity.

Our only wish is that the wishes of our
   long-suffering friends are granted.

Inside me

It Was a Night

Robert van der Valk
South Africa, b. 1951

it
was
a
night
when
i
sat
(alone)
and
wrote
(of
my
eager
lilting
thoughts).

The Mesh

Kwesi Brew
Ghana, b. 1928

We have come to the cross-roads
And I must either leave or come with you.
I lingered over the choice
But in the darkness of my doubts
You lifted the lamp of love
And I saw in your face
The road that I should take

Presentiments

Stephen Watson from the /Xam
South Africa, b. 1954

A presentiment
is that thing which we fear
when something is happening,
near or far, at some other place.

A presentiment is like
a dream which we dream.

Sometimes
when we are alone,
our body starts up, shaken –
it seems as if, to the body,
something was there
which the body feared.

And we pass it,
we who are /Xam,
because our body is telling us:
there is danger at that place.

Confession

Chris van Wyk
South Africa, b. 1957

i would
have brought
you
mulberries
but
they threatened
to explode
their mauve
corpuscles
all over
my
best shirt
so
i ate them

Spell to Banish Fear

Jeni Couzyn
South Africa, b. 1942

By the warmth of the sun
By the baby's cry
By the lambs on the hill
I banish thee.

By the sweetness of the song
By the warm rain falling
By the hum of grass
Begone.

It's Like

Emmanuel Manyindo
Uganda, b. 1973

It's like a lion at your door,
And when your door begins to crack,
It's like a stick across your back,
And when your back begins to smart,
It's like a penknife in your heart,
And when your heart begins to bleed,
You are dead and dead and dead indeed.

It's Always Too Late

Goodintent Mdlalose
South Africa

It's always too late
For us to go back and undo
The damage that we've done
To another person's heart.

It's always too late
To go and thank a person
Who was good to us
And we didn't thank him
When he was still walking on earth.

It's always too late
When we realize
That somebody loved us
And we kept our distance
But now, when we want to go back,
It's too late.

This Is It Man

I R Duncan-Brown
South Africa

This is it man
this is it
a roaring
in your ear –
time is creeping
up your backbone.

You're as Distant as the Moon

Karen Press
South Africa, b. 1956

You're as distant as the moon
Turning turning your dark side
To me

And I just stand there
Howling like a hungry wolf
Growing colder from the feet up

Look how your light is flooding out
Onto her
It's not fair

I'm going to find myself a sun
Full of real light
Come back to dazzle you

And when you come too close
I'll turn into a tiger
Eat you up, roaring

Certainly

Paddi Clay
South Africa, b. 1954

I am happy
when the music
lifts the corner
of your mouth
and you smile
Your hand is very
warm in mine
And you love me

Where the Rainbow Ends

Richard Rive
South Africa, 1931–89

Where the rainbow ends,
There's going to be a place brother,
Where the world can sing all sorts of songs,
And we're going to sing together, brother,
You and I.
Though you're White and I'm not.
It's going to be a sad song, brother,
'Cause we don't know the tune,
And it's a difficult tune to learn,
But we can learn it, brother,
You and I.
There's no such tune as a Black tune,
There's no such tune as a White tune,
There's only music, brother,
And it's the music we're going to sing,
Where the rainbow ends.

117

Me, Coloured

Peter Abrahams
South Africa, b. 1919

Aunt Liza.
Yes?
What am I?
What are you talking about?
I met a boy at the river.
He said he was Zulu.
         She laughed.

You are Coloured.
There are three kinds of people:
White people, Coloured people,
and Black people.
The White people come first,
then the Coloured people,
then the Black people.
Why?
Because it is so.

Next day when I met Joseph,
I smacked my chest and said:
         Me, Coloured!
He clapped his hands and laughed.
Joseph and I spent most
of the long summer afternoons together.
He learned some Afrikaans from me.
I learned some Zulu from him.
Our days were full.
There was the river to explore.
There were my swimming lessons.
I learned to fight with sticks;
to weave a green hat
of the young wands and leaves;
to catch frogs and tadpoles
with my hands;

to set a trap for the *springhaas*;
to make the sounds of the river birds.
There was the hot sun to comfort us.
There was the green grass to dry our bodies.
There was the soft clay with which to build.
There was the fine sand with which to fight.
There were our giant grasshoppers to race.
There were the locust swarms
when the skies turned black
and we caught them by the hundreds.
There was the rare taste of crisp,
brown-baked, salted locusts.
There was the voice of the wind in the willows.
There was the voice of the heavens
in the thunder storms.
There were the voices of two children
in laughter, ours.
There were Joseph's tales of black kings
who lived in days before the white man.
At home, I said:
Aunt Liza?
Yes?
Did we have coloured kings before the white man?
No.
Then where did we come from?
Joseph and his mother come from the
black kings who were before the white man.

Laughing and ruffling my head, she said:
You talk too much. Go 'n wash up.

Apple

Zureida Garda
South Africa

the other day
     I engraved my name
into the flesh
     of an apple.
It looked so bold,
     so definite,
     so permanent.
And yet,
     after I had eaten
          the apple
there was nothing
     left to
     ensure
my existence.

Signature

Shabban Roberts
Tanzania, 1909–62

I am an honest African,
Do not think of me otherwise.
I am not of mixed lineage,
Neither on my mother's nor my father's side.
However fine other lineage may be,
I am not sprung from it.
I am no Arab nor a European,
I am not of Indian descent.
I tell this to the world
So that the curious may know.

A Bird Flew into My Room

Christine Bishop
South Africa, b. 1954

A bird flew into my room and
a drifting feather brushed past my face.
    I was set alight,
    the sensation ran through me
and I couldn't keep it still,
I couldn't hold it in
and I had to burst forward
    and catch that feather
and feel that tenderness
            just one more time.

A Thought

Graham Lazar
South Africa, b. 1956

it's just occurred that something blurred
is coming over me.
it isn't funny, or sad, it's just plain goddam mad.
it's a feeling, it's buzzing around in my head.
trying to tell me something, but i don't understand
its language.
pity, i was looking forward to knowing.

The Web

Michele James
South Africa, b.1955

i remember
when i was a little girl
i pressed my nose
against the window-pane
and watched
a silver drop of rain
and i smiled ...

and i saw
a spider
scuttling
toward me
and the world was
new and perfect
and i laughed ...

but i grew up
and the rain was channeled
into one huge roaring sea
and it closed around me
i grasped at
nothingness
i was helpless
and i struggled blindly
into the trap
and i was entangled
in the web
there was no escape
the world was dark and terrifying
and i cried ...

Reluctance

Mxolisi Nyezwa
South Africa, b. 1967

the night is the night
final
the day is the day
final

I am neither of the two
it's that simple

final

Self-examination

Lechesa Tsenoli
South Africa

I need a mirror, desperately
To see myself, my reflection;
To see the reality that I am.

I long to see my eyes;
To read the tales they tell
To others looking at me;
To decipher the puzzle
That I am.

My Black Skin

Shepistone Sekeso
Zimbabwe

You are as dark
And as lovely
As the silent night.
I am proud of you.
You are as lovely
As a ripened grape,
Smooth and dark.
You are a perfect cover.
You fit me well,
My black skin.

I Can't Ever Forget

Robert van der Valk
South Africa, b. 1951

i can't ever forget
the time
when, as a child,
i was assured;
the time
when, in my heart,
i felt secure.
and now, as one who has not forgotten,
i stand,
often alone,
i stand
undecided.
yet, deeper, far beneath,
i feel a further me:
a someone.
and in myself
i seek my reassurance;
the reassurance
i cannot reach.
i may be happy,
yet sadness is my watchword.
there is a better kind
and in my mind
i am the image
of that me.
there is no regret.
no grudge.
still there is something,
far away,
i cannot reach.
i cannot reach
myself.

Feeling Sad

Kate Boswell
South Africa, b. 1972

Feeling sad,
Look at my feet,
Think: maybe if I keep my head down
No one will notice me.
Pretend interest in shoe.
Hot eyes and cheeks burn
Fire joins water
Panic!
Frantically blink
Breathe in deep
Think: can't cry now ...
Raise the eyebrows
But
Tears swell and spill,
Slowly slide uncontrollably
Down fiery cheeks
Leaving wet tracks.

The Nightmare

Roisin McCarthy
Lesotho, b. 1972

Walking through the graveyard
Death is in the air,
Tripping over in the darkness
Over deadly looking graves,
Blood gurgling screams of pain
Come to my frozen ears,
Sounds of splattering everywhere,
As the axe cuts right through.
Footsteps behind me come closer and closer
The shadow of an axe behind me
Coming for my head …
AARGH!!
Whew, it's only a dream!

Animals

ETOSHA PAN WILD LIFE.

© 1982 JOHN N. MUAFANGEJO.

Blue Mist Like Smoke

Stephen Watson from the /Xam
South Africa, b. 1954

The hare
is like a mist,
like !kho,
a blue mist
resembling smoke,
our mothers used to say.

When a mirage
appears at daybreak,
just before sunrise,
they say it is
the hare,
the mirage in it,
that keeps the sun in mist,
that cloaks the sun in smoke.
that weakens the sun's eye,
that does not let it rise,
and brings much illness
to us.

It is, they say,
the hare that does it,
a hare like mist,
a hare like smoke,
the mirage in it,
the !kho of it.

It is, they say,
a smoke resembling mist,
blue mist like smoke
that does it.

The Earth I Tread Upon

Lazarus D K Dokora
Zimbabwe

a tortoise wish

Not my fault that
I carry about me
My bedroom eternal.

Not my desire
That I move forward
Like I'm reversing.

But my ancient custom
Is never to hasten hastily,
Nor to lag far behind.

I keep watching this:
My country-side and the air,
And the earth I tread upon.

Sailing Alone Around the World

Gus Ferguson
South Africa, b. 1940

for Lauren

In Cape Town many years ago
There lived a snail called Dallio
'Though slow as often molluscs are

130

He yearned and burned to travel far.

He had no kids, he had no wife
And travelled all his livelong life.
His meals he took while on the hoof,
His shell, a backpack and a roof.

He tacked in six years all the way
From Rocklands Beach to Bantry Bay.
Long-suffering, with motives pure,
He learned, while living, to endure.

Then, on his death, his soul was told:
"Obsessive snail, since you were bold,
The doughtiest of all your nation,
You can choose your re-incarnation."

"Ironical," old Dallio said,
"Alive I had no choice, but dead
An option looms, I'll be a man,
A great explorer if I can,

And circumnavigate the Earth.
Around its plumply massive girth
I'll sail, alone, by night and day
Through wave and wind, in storm and spray

In a solo sloop of wood and oakum.
And can I be called, please, Joshua Slocum?"

Footnote: Coincidentally a certain Joshua Slocum did sail his sloop, the 'Spray', alone around the world and in 1900 published a book about it, which has the same title as this poem.

Limerick

Gus Ferguson
South Africa, b. 1940

There once was a poet called: Gus
Who made an ecological fuss.
He'd rant and he'd rail
On the rights of the snail
'Til his lettuce cried: "What about us?!"

Familiar Oxen

Oumar Ba
Mauretania, 1900-?

You tell me you have right on your side?
And those oxen that I see
In the chief's herd?
If I call them
They will respond to their baptismal names.

Detachment

I R Duncan-Brown
South Africa

Stumpy sunrise dog
at quarter to seven
walking with your
outrageous flag of a tail
at such a jaunty angle ...
you're so close to the ground
that you can't get above it all
and see it in perspective –
but we have no such excuse.

Two Dogs on the Beach

Nibor Nalam
South Africa, b. 1940

In the distance I can see the Sit Boys,
two large black dogs who rush up dunes
and turn and charge down into waves.
One call or whistle from their human
as I even distantly approach
and the Sit Boys lollop over to him, sit,
and lift their heads to receive their leads.
They wag their tails as if they like being led
almost as much as they like being free.

Bird

Ruth Jacobson
South Africa

I love you, sunlit freckled
Speckled brown bird
Picking and pecking
Down in the dust
In the warm, warm, welcoming
Dry red dust,
In the blanket of sun
(Under yellow, yellow sunflowers)
Picking and pecking
Your speck of the world.

Guinea Fowl

Candy Neubert
South Africa

Where are the guinea fowl?
I don't know.
Who can guess
Where the guinea fowl go?

Just outside
By the mulberry tree,
That's where the guinea fowl
Used to be.

They had blue heads
And little white spots;
I saw seven guinea fowl
– That's lots.

I knew them
And they all knew me,
And they all lived
In the mulberry tree.

Now there are three
New buildings there,
Instead of the grass
And weeds and air.

Someone's wall
Round the tree next door
Which hadn't been anyone's
Tree before.

Diggers and trucks
Drive by all day,
That's why the guinea fowl
Went away.

People need homes
And if that's true,
I hope the guinea fowl
Find homes too.

I always look
Wherever we go –
Where are the guinea fowl?
I don't know.

The End of Green Baboon

Dambudzo Marechera
Zimbabwe, 1952–87

Once upon a time
In a town at the end of the rainbow
There lived a black baboon
And a white baboon
And a green baboon

It was very hot
The sun was bloodshot
There was not a drop of rain
"Drought!" shouted the *Daily Baboon* newspaper

Black baboon was hungry. Very hungry.
White Baboon was very very hungry.
Green Baboon was also hungry.
"There is nothing but hunger at the end
Of the rainbow," said the *Daily Baboon* newspaper.

Black Baboon heard a voice.
The voice was the voice of his hunger.
The voice was coming from his stomach.
"A is Awful, B is Baboonery, and C is Cad!" said the voice.
"Shut up!" cried Black Baboon, "Shut up!"
White Baboon was walking down the street.
He stopped and listened. He leaned over the gate.
Black Baboon was shouting, "Shut up! Shut up!"
White Baboon was very angry. He jumped over the gate.
He hit Black Baboon on the head.

Black Baboon forgot the voice of his hunger.
Black Baboon hit White Baboon. They fought. They bit.
They hit. They smashed. They scratched. They snarled.
Green Baboon was passing by. "Stop!" he screamed, "Please
    stop!"
"What did you say?" said Black Baboon and White
Baboon together, "What did you say?"
"Please don't fight," said Green Baboon, "I can't stand it!"
Black Baboon looked at White Baboon.
White Baboon looked at Black Baboon.
They both looked at Green Baboon.
Their eyes were small and sharp.

"No!" screamed Green Baboon, "No, don't!"
Green Baboon was very afraid. "No! No − ohh!"
Black Baboon looked at White Baboon.
White Baboon looked at Black Baboon.
They looked at Green Baboon.
Their eyes were small and sharp.

They jumped on Green Baboon.
They hit. They bit. They scratched. They beat him up.
They hit him the whole day. It was like thunder.
The rainbow drained of all colour.
Black Baboon and White Baboon were eating Green Baboon.
White Baboon liked his Green Baboon with garlic.

Black Baboon liked his Green Baboon with chillies.

"Let us eat him in a civilised way," said White Baboon.
Black Baboon agreed, "Let us eat him in a civilised way."
They carried Green Baboon into the kitchen.
They cut Green Baboon into chops and steaks.
They cooked Green Baboon with spices and dry white wine.
White Baboon made the salad.
Black Baboon made the custard.

They spread the tablecloth on the table out on the verandah.
They set the knives and forks. They placed two plates
And two serviettes and two comfortable chairs.
They sat down to eat. The moon was up, big and round.
Black Baboon put on a record on the gramaphone.
"Ah, Beethoven!" sighed White Baboon listening to the music.

It was beautiful.
It was romantic.
It was the end of Green Baboon.

Lizard

Nguni Muchaka
South Africa

He lay dazzled,
Trying to watch the birds,
But blinded by the sun.

The Snake Song

John Mbiti
Kenya

Neither legs nor arms have I
But I crawl on my belly
And I have
Venom, venom, venom!

Neither horns nor hoofs have I
But I spit with my tongue
And I have
Venom, venom, venom!

Neither bows nor guns have I
But I flash fast my tongue
And I have
Venom, venom, venom!

Neither radar nor missiles have I
But I stare with my eyes
And I have
Venom, venom, venom!

I master every movement
For I jump, run and swim
and I spit
Venom, venom, venom!

Chameleon

Mudereri Khadani
Zimbabwe, b. 1952

Not fast – now –
Not so fast –
You see –
Calculate –
And –
And Estimate –
Then –
Carefully now –
Experiment –
No! no! no!
Hesitate –
Now then –
Grope – and reach –
That's right.
You gotta be sure
The world's welcome's sure.

Grandma used to tell me
Go slow and don't show,
Look how chameleon does it,
Gradually,
Everything all in time.
But then she forgot
Chameleons change
Tactics with circumstance
Even down to appearance.
They abandon custom
When the need changes.
Ever watched its tongue attack?

The Frog

Mavis Smallberg
South Africa, b. 1940s

I wake to faint soft shuffling
of insistent feet.
Drowsily I peer over the bed's edge:
There, a dainty little frog
brown speckled,
with beady pinhead eyes
blackbright
sits in frog position
on the floor

So frog
you too, like moth and man,
hanker after light.
And now, with tiny silly leaps,
you try to reach the globe
just above the floor

What am I to do?
I cannot sleep with you so
close about my head.
What if with one supreme athletic leap
you land upon my face?
What if you should light upon my sheet
And I awake to find
the shiny up-side-down frog shape
imprinted on my cheek?

I know:
The Cat!
I open up the door;
she comes sniff-sniffing in.
Oh! she knows about your presence, then
I move the bed
to lighten, ease her task.

Sorry, Frog.
You hop,
I leap upon the bed.
I cannot bear to see you crushed,
I do not really want you dead.
But I cannot
have you in my bed!

With swishing tail
she taps and waits.
You do not move
you're playing dead!
She yawns and settles down to wait.
That's just not fair!
It's nearly four
and still you sit froglike
upon my floor!

I read a book.
My feline friend is dozing off,
and whisper-soft you move away –
I know what I will do:
I'll take a bucket with which I'll cover you.
Tomorrow, when my braver friends awake,
they'll set you free
and I will smile and tell them
how you pestered me.

I stand
poised with bucket
in my hand ...
You hop
I leap –
My feet!

You disappear behind an empty shoe.
Dear Frog,
I've had enough and so have you.

You're miles now from my bed.
The cat's asleep upon her paw.
I'll shut the light
and in the darkness that ensues,
we both will sleep and
darkly dream
how light might mark
our freedom in
the morning.

A Newly Born Calf

Mbuyiseni Oswald Mtshali
South Africa, b. 1940

A newly born calf
is like oven-baked bread
steaming under a cellophane cover.
The cow cuts
the shiny coat
as a child would
lick a toffee
with a tongue as pink as
the sole of a foot.
The calf sways on legs
filled with jelly and custard
instead of bone and marrow;
and it totters
to suck the teats
of its mother's udder.

It's Fun

Dennis Brutus
South Africa, b. 1924

for Justin who asked for a dolphin poem

It's fun
in the sun
and cool
in the pool
with pleasant shadows
to hide away
and I never know need
with a regular feed
at special times every day

But oh to be free
in the wide open sea
roaming the ocean meadows
or to laze in the bay
and gambol all day

To be free, to be free, to be free!

Poetry

Wha-Yong Lee
Botswana, b. 1975

Writing poetry is like watching
a dove in the park. In the far corner
close by the swings, a dove, twitching and
picking from the earthen ground,
it looks for its usual one pound
worm.

From the high acorn trees
it dives down like an arrow,
flutters down to bathe its
turquoise wings in the fountain waves.
It looks with its crystal eyes
and backs upon its wings,
thrashes the air and is gone.

Index of poets

Acknowledgements

The compiler and the publishers are grateful for permission for use in Africa south of the Sahara of copyright material in this book as follows:

Beverley Abel for 'Suns' from *The Capetonian* (Cape Town High School, 1971); Jessica Abrahams for 'Windy Morning' & 'Stay You Well' from *The Capetonian* (Cape Town High School, 1971 & 1973); The Estate of Peter Abrahams for 'Me, Coloured' from *Tell Freedom* (permission granted by Faber & Faber Ltd); G Adali-Morti for 'Palm Leaves of Childhood' from *Poems from Black Africa* (Indiana University Press, 1963); Ama Ata Aidoo for 'Dilemma of a Ghost' from *African Poetry for Schools 1* (Longman, 1978); John S Ambrose and Muzi Maziya for 'The Only Wish' from *Phoenix* (Waterford Kamhlaba UWCSA, 1986); Jared Angira for 'The Sprinter' from *Silent Voices* (Heinemann); Tyrone August for 'One Day' from *Staffrider* Vol 9 No 1 (COSAW, 1990); Oumar Ba for 'Familiar Oxen'; Roberick Baard for 'The 800 Metres' from *The Capetonian* (Cape Town High School, 1970); Cathy Bell for 'Innocence' from *English Alive* (SACEE, 1969); Christine Bishop for 'A Bird Flew into My Room' from *The Capetonian* (Cape Town High School, 1971); Ralph Bitamazire for his translation of the traditional 'The Poet to His Readers'; Kate Boswell for 'Feeling Sad' from *Phoenix* (Waterford Kamhlaba UWCSA, 1985); Martin Brennan for 'Ali the Driver' from *Poems for Africa* (Blackie & Son); Kwesi Brew for 'The Mesh'; B N Brink for 'Fear' from *English Alive* (SACEE, 1969); Pip Broadbent for 'No Letters Yet' from *English Alive* (SACEE, 1969); Dennis Brutus for 'It's Fun' from *Stubborn Hope* (Heinemann, 1978); Masautso Chaponda for 'What They Say about Pickles' from *Phoenix* (Waterford Kamhlaba UWCSA, 1988); Taziona Chaponda for 'My Shoes' from *Phoenix* (Waterford Kamhlaba UWCSA, 1990); Julius Chingono for 'My Old Shoe' & 'An Epitaph' from *Zimbabwean Poetry in English* (Mambo Press, 1978); Shimmer Chinodya for 'Wild Mushroom'; I Choonara for 'Upside-Down Cake'; John Pepper Clark-Bekederemo for 'Ibadan' & 'Streamside Exchange'; Peter E Clarke for 'Beachcombing', 'Bookshelf', 'Oupa's Chair', 'Registering for School, 1936', 'Small Bench', & 'Young Shepherd Bathing His Feet'; Paddi Clay for 'Certainly' from *The Capetonian* (Cape Town High School, 1970); Jeni Couzyn for 'Spring Song' & 'Spell to Banish Fear' from *Life by Drowning* (Anansi, 1983); Jose Craveirinha for 'Fable' from *Staffrider* Vol 11 (COSAW, 1993); Colin Dalziel for 'As I Went Home from School' from *The Capetonian* (Cape Town High School, 1968); Jane Dederick for 'Jacobus' by Robert Dederick; Ingrid de Kok for 'Stones Sky Radio' from *Familiar Ground* (Ravan, 1988); Peter Delius for 'Emerald Dove' by Anthony Delius from *A Corner of the World* (Human & Rousseau, 1962); Prashant Desai for 'Poem' from *Phoenix* (Waterford Kamhlaba UWCSA, 1989); Nomsa Dlamini for 'I Wonder' from *Phoenix* (Waterford Kamhlaba UWCSA, 1982); Lazarus D K Dokora for 'The Earth I Tread Upon' from *And Now the Poets Speak* (Mambo Press, 1981); I R Duncan-Brown for 'This Is It, Man' & 'Detachment' from *English Alive* (SACEE, 1970); Louise Eyeington for 'The Fade of Day' & 'On Holiday' from *Phoenix* (Waterford Kamhlaba UWCSA, 1985); Said Farah for 'The Wind' from *Phoenix* (Waterford Kamhlaba UWCSA, 1988); Gus Ferguson for 'Limerick' & 'Sailing Alone Around the World'; Mark Finkenstein for 'Me (or Soccer in the Street)' from *The Capetonian* (Cape Town High School, 1968); Michele Freind for 'Days' & 'Peak Hour' from *The Capetonian* (Cape Town High School, 1970); (The Estate of Shirley Futeran for 'To a Sleeping Child' from *The Capetonian* (Cape Town High School, 1971); Zureida Garda for 'Apple' from *English Alive* (SACEE, 1991); Joseph Gatuiria for 'Kariuki' from *Poetry Anthology for Junior Secondary Schools* (Macmillan Press Ltd, 1978); Jeremy Gordin for 'Little Girl', 'Into Sleep' & 'Yeoville Park, 1986'; Denzil Gunning for 'The Shell' from *The Capetonian* (Cape Town High School, 1968); Chenjerai Hove for 'Exiled Farmer'; J O Ige for 'The Poet to His Readers'; Jeanette Isaacman for 'Ignorance' from *The Capetonian* (Cape Town High School, 1971); Ruth Jacobson for 'Pear' & 'Bird' from *English Alive* (SACEE, 1970); Michele James for 'The Web' from *The Capetonian* (Cape Town High School, 1970); Wopko Jensma for 'Not Him: Section 3' from *Sing for Our Execution* (Ravan, 1973); Gavin Kaplan for 'The Fair' from *The Capetonian* (Cape Town High School, 1970); Mudereri Khadani for 'Chameleon' from *The Mambo Book of Zimbabwean Verse in English* (Mambo Press, 1978); Elizabeth Khaxas for 'Okombahe' from *Staffrider* Vol 11 (COSAW, 1993); Michael Kuus for 'The Goey-Gumdy' from *The Capetonian* (Cape Town High School, 1968); Susan Latimer for 'A Little Man' from *The Capetonian* (Cape Town High School, 1973); Graham Lazar for 'A Thought' from *The Capetonian* (Cape Town High School, 1970); Wha-Yong Lee for 'Poetry' from *Phoenix* (Waterford Kamhlaba UWCSA, 1989); Bernard Levinson for 'Elsie' from *From Breakfast to Madness* (Ravan, 1974); Ronald H Louw for 'Away from the Rain' from *English Alive* (SACEE, 1975); Trevor Lubbe for 'The Burglar' from *English Alive* (SACEE, 1970); S Lubega for 'Two Men and the Axe' from *Poetry Anthology for Junior Secondary Schools* (Macmillan Pres Ltd, 1978); Ayanda Madide for 'The Untold Dream' from *English Alive* (SACEE, 1989); Mpho

Mamashela for 'The Mist' from *Phoenix* (Waterford Kamhlaba UWCSA, 1980); Emmanuel Manyindo for 'It's Like' from *Phoenix* (Waterford Kamhlaba UWCSA, 1986); Heinemann Publishers, Oxford for 'The Sweet Brew at Chitakale' by Jack Mapanje from *Of Chameleons and Gods* (Heinemann Educational Books, 1981); Dambudzo Marechera Trust for 'The End of Green Baboon, Part One' from *Scrapiron Blues* (Baobab Books, 1994); Ilda Maria for 'Cookology First, Biology Second' from *Breakfast of Sjamboks* (Zimbabwe Publishing House, 1987); Eric Mazani for 'My Grandmother is My Love' from *Zimbabwean Poetry in English* (Mambo Press, 1978); Muzi Maziya and John Ambrose from 'The Only Wish' from *Phoenix* (Waterford Kamhlaba UWCSA, 1986); John Mbiti for 'The Snake Song' from *My World* (David Philip); Roisin McCarthy for 'The Nightmare' from *Phoenix* (Waterford Kamhlaba UWCSA, 1985); Goodintent Mdlalose for 'It's Always Too Late' from *English Alive* (SACEE, 1989); Dikobe wa Mogale and Ad Donker Publishers for 'A Conversation with My Son' from *Prison Poems* (Ad Donker Publishers, 1992); Seitlhamo Motsapi for 'The House' from *New Coin*, Vol 30 No 1 (ISEA, Rhodes University, June 1994); Oswald Mtshali for 'A Newly Born Calf' & 'Inside My Zulu Hut' from *Sounds of a Cowhide Drum* (Ad Donker Publishers, 1972); Nguni Muchaka for 'Lizard' from *English Alive* (SACEE, 1983); Charles Mungoshi for 'Dotito is Our Brother', 'One for the Road' & 'Pioneer Street is Dying' (Zimbabwe Poetry Society); Colin Muskett for 'The High Jump' from *The Capetonian* (Cape Town High School, 1970); Mteto Mzongwana for 'Old Age' from *My Music My Love* (Snailpress, 1993); Nibor Nalam for 'Going up Going Down', 'Hey Man I'm the Same Mpho!', 'Nothing There!', 'School Visit', 'Sitting on a Rock', '6-Hour Time Difference', 'Two Dogs on a Beach' & 'Ithemba Alibulali'; Ntsieni N Ndou for 'City-bound Train' from *Staffrider* Vol 2 No 1 (Ravan, 1979); Candy Neubert for 'Guinea Fowl' & 'The Smart Shoe'; Lizzie Ngwenya for 'Dusk in Africa' from *Phoenix* (Waterford Kamhlaba UWCSA, 1986); Motshile wa Nthodi for 'Song of the Stick Fighter' from *Blue Black & Other Poems*; Nyezwa Mxolisi for 'Reluctance' from *Essential Things* (COSAW, 1992); Michael O'Hara for 'Wind' from *Phoenix* (Waterford Kamhlaba UWCSA, 1982); Albert Ojuka for 'Pedestrian to Passing Benz-Man' from *Uhuru's Fire* (Cambridge University Press, 1977); Atukwei Okai for 'Jonice' from *Poems of Black Africa* (Heinemann, 1975); Estate of Okot p'Bitek for extract from 'Song of Ocol' and for 'The Graceful Giraffe cannot become a Monkey' & 'There Is No Fixed Time for Breast-feeding', extracts from *Song of Lawino* (Heinemann, 1984); Dele Olaniyi for 'Verbs' from *Poetry Anthology for Junior Secondary Schools* (Macmillan Press Ltd, 1978); Essop Patel for 'Moon a Balloon' from *Exiles Within* (Writers' Forum, 1986); Kathryn Phelan for 'Jealousy' from *English Alive* (SACEE, 1986); Michael Powell for 'My Home that Would Never Exist' from *The Capetonian* (Cape Town High School, 1968); Karen Press for 'Cape Flats', 'Beds', 'You're as Distant as the Moon', 'To a Class of Test-writers', 'Things I Have Seen', & 'She Brought Home Poppies'; Estate of Richard Rive and David Philip Publishers for 'Where the Rainbow Ends'; Shabban Roberts for 'Signature'; Heather Robertson for 'Under the Sun'; Acelio Ruface for 'I Hear Silent Steps' from *Breakfast of Sjamboks* (Zimbabwe Publishing House, 1987); Shepistone Sekeso for 'My Black Skin' from *Mambo Book of Zimbabwean Verse in English* (Mambo Press, 1986); Colin Sentongo for 'Poem: The School Bus' from *Phoenix* (Waterford Kamhlaba UWCSA, 1986); Adam Small for 'Brown Lullaby'; Mavis Smallberg for 'The Frog' from *Essential Things* (COSAW, 1992); Daniel Stolfi for 'An Old Uncle's Vegetable Garden' from *Vectors* (Snailpress, 1992); Michael Strauss for 'Tribute to a Boy' from *English Alive* (SACEE, 1969); Stuart Stromin for 'Joy' from *English Alive* (SACEE, 1975); Shelley Swade for 'Hey Beggar' from *English Alive* (SACEE, 1969); Thabang Thoka for 'Two Worlds' from *Phoenix* (Waterford Kamhlaba UWCSA, 1979); Lechesa Tsenoli for 'Self-examination' from *Staffrider* Vol 2 No 3; Robert van der Valk for 'I Saw Her There One Day', 'Happy Little Boy', 'I Can't Ever Forget', 'It Was a Night', & 'I Watched Him' from *The Capetonian* (Cape Town High School, 1969); Esther van der Vyver for 'Emily' from *English Alive* (SACEE,1987); Chris van Wyk for 'Confession' from *It Is Time to Go Home* (Ad Donker, 1979); Jennifer Venter for 'Eternity' from *English Alive* (SACEE, 1974); Stephen Watson for 'Presentiments', 'The Sound of the Stars', 'The Name of My Place', 'Catching a Porcupine' & 'Blue Mist Like Smoke'; Nonhlanhla Shembe Williams for 'My Strange Room' from *Phoenix* (Waterford Kamhlaba UWCSA, 1986); Musaemura Zimunya for 'Ask Grandpa' and 'Children's Rain Song'.

Every effort has been made to trace and acknowledge copyright holders. Should any mistake or omission have been made, the publishers and compiler apologise and will correct it in the next impression.

Other books compiled by Robin Malan

Poetry

EXPLORINGS (David Philip Cape Town 1988)
POETRY WORKS 1 (David Philip Cape Town 1995)
POETRY WORKS 2 (David Philip Cape Town forthcoming)
INSCAPES (Oxford University Press Southern Africa Cape Town 1969)
NEW INSCAPES (Oxford University Press Southern Africa Cape Town 1986)
WORLDSCAPES (Oxford University Press Southern Africa Cape Town forthcoming)
OUTRIDINGS (Oxford University Press Southern Africa Cape Town 1972)
NEW OUTRIDINGS (Oxford University Press Southern Africa Cape Town 1993)

Short Stories

BEING HERE (David Philip Cape Town 1994)
NEW BEGINNINGS (Oxford University Press Southern Africa Cape Town 1995)

Plays

PLAY WORKSHOP (Oxford University Press Southern Africa 1972)
THE DISTANCE REMAINS AND OTHER PLAYS (Oxford University Press Southern Africa Cape Town 1996)

Mixed Genre

OURSELVES IN SOUTHERN AFRICA (Macmillan London 1988)